There Was Before I Loved You, But Never an After

Ariella Tabaković

To the reader,

I began writing this book during what felt like the brightest chapter of my life, a time when I was surrounded by a love I never knew existed. This book is, at its core, a testament to love, to its joy, its heartbreak, and everything in between.

As you turn these pages, I hope you find pieces of your own story. Maybe you'll remember your first love or recognize how love can both lift us up and break us apart in ways we never expected. Love is messy, imperfect, but it connects us and teaches us what it means to truly live.

This story isn't just mine anymore. It's ours now, to carry, to feel, and to remember.

With love,
From me to you.

Copyright & Publishing Info

Publisher: BoD · Books on Demand, Strandvejen 100,
2900 Hellerup, bod@bod.dk
Print: Libri Plureos GmbH, Friedensallee 273,
22763 Hamborg, Tyskland
ISBN: 978-87-7145-698-1

For The Boy Named After A Fairytale

I never cared for the scent of lavender, but when you told me it was your favorite flower, I wanted to fill my entire backyard with fields of its purple blooms.

Part One

The Innocence of Love

Everything I Knew About Life As A Child

I grew up in a small town with religious parents, which basically meant my life came with a script I didn't write and rules I wasn't allowed to question. Every decision, every thought, had a guideline. Some were spoken, others just quietly understood, like they'd been passed down and etched into stone. Even love wasn't just love. It had a checklist. It had to be pure, patient, saved for the right person, someone who was worthy. And it had to fit into this perfect little future. Faith, family, Sunday mornings in church, hand in hand with your spouse under the watchful eyes of the congregation.

At least, that's what my mother believed, what she wanted for me. And in a town like ours, there was no such thing as privacy. One thing I'll never forget is how impossible it was to go unnoticed. If someone didn't see you, they heard about you. And if they didn't hear the truth, they'd just make it up or let the neighbors fill in the blanks. I remember once, I walked to the store, just minding my own business, and by the time I got home, my mom already knew. "Oh, Lilly, I just saw your daughter heading downtown," someone had told her, smiling in that too sweet, too knowing way. It was like the whole town had eyes. Like living in a fishbowl where everyone had a front row seat and a megaphone.

My parents, who were and still are deeply religious, never let me forget that my life was supposed to have meaning. That God had a plan, and it was my job to follow it. Love, marriage, family, faith. It was all part of one long, holy line I was expected to walk. From baptism to heaven, no detours. Anything outside of that wasn't just wrong. It was temptation. And since we lived in a town where everyone knew everyone's business, my parents were always reminding me to be careful. Careful how I dressed. Careful what I said. Careful who I spent time with.

"You don't want to embarrass yourself or us," they'd say. And *"People talk"* became less of a warning and more like a mantra. Something that lived in the back of my mind, echoing even when no one was around. Even when it came to friendships, my parents kept a close eye on who I spent time with. They were always reminding me that the people I surrounded myself with would reflect not just on me, but on them too. *"Be careful who you call your friends," they* would say. *"If they act foolishly, it will reflect poorly on you as well."* In the end, it was never really about staying out of trouble. It was about maintaining a certain image. One that matched the expectations of the church and the standards of our community. I was supposed to look neat and modest, act polite and respectful, and never, under any circumstances, draw the wrong kind of attention.

"Think of how you will be perceived." That thought followed me everywhere.

Even though I tried to follow every rule my parents laid out for me, I could never seem to fit perfectly into the path they had imagined. My parents longed for the picture-perfect daughter. The girl who smiled sweetly, wore soft and delicate clothes, and dreamed of a life centered around family, church, and finding the one. But I was not that girl. I was not the pretty pink princess they hoped for. Not because I was rebellious or trying to turn away from God. I still believed in something greater than myself. But I needed to find out who I was before I became what they wanted me to be. Before I could walk that path, I had to know if it was mine to begin with. But that was not something I was allowed to do.

Asking questions about identity, needing space to figure things out on my own, exploring my own dreams, it all felt like betrayal in my house. Everything had already been planned. How I should look. Who I should be around. What kind of life I should want. There was no space for anything different.

And so, I felt alone. Completely alone.

My house, in many ways, became a kind of prison. Not because my parents were cruel. They were not. They just cared so deeply that their love came with too many conditions. Conditions that wrapped around me so tightly that I could barely breathe. I was not allowed to go anywhere unless it was supervised. Even then, my mom would be ten steps behind me, watching closely. There were strict boundaries. No sleepovers. No hanging out at the mall after school. My world existed within the four walls of our house, and my bedroom became my cell. I would spend hours lying in bed, staring at the ceiling, imagining a life that felt bigger than the one I was living. But I had my phone. My iPad. I would scroll endlessly through YouTube, watching people who seemed to be truly alive. Travel vloggers visiting Seoul, Tokyo, New York, cities I could only dream about. Their lives looked so vibrant, so full of freedom and choices they made for themselves. And it wasn't that I wanted to leave everything my parents believed in. I didn't want to leave them behind either. I just wanted to breathe. Just for a moment. I wanted to find out who I was outside of the rules, the expectations, the constant pressure to fit into a mold that never quite felt like mine.

But I sometimes did wonder if I was wrong for wanting more. My parents always told me I should be content with the life God gave me. That too much independence, too much ambition, was dangerous.

"The world is full of temptation."

"Stay grounded, or you'll lose yourself."

But what if what I needed was to lose myself, just for a little while, to finally find out who I really was?

I felt like I didn't belong anywhere. My town was too small. My home was too restrictive. And my dreams felt too big. So, I kept lying in bed, existing while watching life happen through the glow of my small iPad screen. Time slipped away from me. Each passing moment blurred into the next. Days turned into weeks, and weeks into months. The only thing that changed was how old the iPad was getting, its screen still glowing, still playing the same quiet hum of videos on repeat. The isolation didn't just wear me down. It reshaped me. It made me quieter. More guarded. When you are alone for too long, you start to build walls around yourself.
Not just to keep others out, but to keep yourself safe.
Safe from their expectations.
Safe from their questions.
I ached to break free from the life I was only surviving in, but I had no idea how. Every time I thought about speaking up, about asking for space or freedom or anything more, I could already hear the disappointment in my parents' voices. So, I stayed quiet. I didn't want to be a burden. I didn't want to be a problem. And so, I watched from the sidelines while the world moved on without me.

What more could I have done? I was just a child. A child who wanted to live freely and understand what true happiness felt like.

Love, back then,
was about following rules
and earning smiles
by being quiet, good, controlled.
It meant staying inside the lines
that were drawn for me
without asking why.

But one day,
the rules didn't explain the ache anymore.
And I started wondering,
what if love wasn't something to follow,
but something to feel?

But what if I didn't know how to love?

What if I couldn't be loved?

Everything I Knew About Love As A Teen

Love, at least the romantic kind, was always treated as the most important thing in the world. Everyone talked about it like it was the ultimate goal, the thing that made poets lose their minds and musicians repeat the same three chords about someone's eyes shining bright like the stars. It seemed like life revolved around love, and everyone believed in it. Even as a kid, I thought I understood the basics of it. Fall in love, get married, or at least post cute couple selfies tagged #loml, and then live out the rest of your life holding hands. It was as predictable as gravity, like something Isaac Newton had described.

But I just couldn't wrap my head around why people thought love was worth all the hype. It wasn't just that I had never been in love. I had never even seen it work. My parents split up when I was nine, but then they'd get back together, only to break up again. It was this endless cycle of instability. My dad kept messing up, my mom struggled to find security, and I ended up stuck in the middle, watching them try and fail to make it work. My older brother had relationships that started with laughs but ended with nothing but tears. Even the couples on TV seemed fake, and the whispers between my classmates about their crushes always felt like they were reading lines from some off-screen script.

"Oh my god, John looked at me in biology."

"Jessica wrote his initials in her notebook."

But was that supposed to be love? A glance? A doodle on a piece of paper? I just didn't understand.

Some said I was jealous. But I wasn't. I wasn't sitting there hoping someone would glance my way in biology class. I just couldn't shake the feeling that love was some kind of game everyone swore was real, but whenever I asked my classmates what the rules were, they'd just stare at me blankly. They hadn't grown up with rules attached to it like I had.

And when I think back, there was something that really got under my skin, it was the way people obsessed over love. For this topic, there's no better example than Elen, my best friend since kindergarten. She believed in love the way some people believe in horoscopes. To her, it was this cosmic thing, written somewhere in the stars, and if you just lived your life right, your prince charming would show up exactly when you needed him. She was obsessed. She had been planning her dream wedding since she was ten. It would have flowers, twinkling lights, and the perfect first dance song. What made it even funnier was that she had never actually dated anyone. Still, to her, love was a safe haven. A place where everything made sense.

But to me, love didn't seem safe at all.

When I first started noticing how people acted when they liked someone, it always seemed to mean one thing. It meant touching someone when they didn't want to be touched. It started small. Grabbing a wrist. Poking someone during math class. But then it escalated. Hands on shoulders. Hands on waists. Hands where they shouldn't be. And if you complained, people would just shrug it off. *"He's probably just shy and doesn't know how to say he likes you."* As if touching your thigh or slapping your ass was some kind of love language. As if we were supposed to take it as a compliment. I once overheard a teacher tell a girl, *"You should be flattered. It means he admires you."* As if admiration made it okay. As if it didn't make your skin crawl or leave you wondering whether you had done something wrong just by existing in a way that made someone notice you.

What made it worse were the girls who didn't get mad at the boys. They got mad at you. If you so much as looked at the boy someone else liked, you were labeled a boyfriend thief. It didn't matter that the boy was not someone you even liked. Or that he had cornered you in the library. Or that he had *"accidentally"* brushed his hand against your chest during group projects. To them, it was your fault. You were the threat. And no one likes a girl who's a threat.
Elen used to say those girls were just insecure. *"They're scared,"* she'd explain. *"They think if someone else has what they want, it means they'll never get it themselves."* Maybe she was right. But still, I made myself smaller. I let them corner me. Let them mock me. Let them make me feel like a joke. Because deep down, some part of me believed I had to please them in order to belong.

And it wore me down.

By the time I was fifteen, I only talked to boys when I absolutely had to. Some people probably thought I hated them. Someone once joked, "She's allergic to the male species." But that wasn't the truth. The truth was I just didn't want the drama. The dirty looks. The rumors that would spread before the final bell even rang. It wasn't worth it. None of it really was.
Still, no matter where I turned, love always came with new expectations. It was only seen as real when it fit a certain mold. When it was public. Visible. Romanticized. At school, there was this unspoken timeline you were expected to follow if you wanted to be

seen as someone who understood love. The rules weren't written down, but everyone knew them.

- First, you were supposed to lose your virginity before eighteen, but not too early or you'd be labeled a slut.

- Second, if you didn't have a boyfriend by twenty, people assumed there was something wrong with you.

- Third, marriage could wait, but only after you'd had a bit of fun with a few people. Not too many though, or you'd be judged for that too.

These invisible rules were made up and enforced by the same girls who had been dreaming about love since they were kids, long before any of us fully understood what it meant.

Even with all that, I still wanted to believe love wasn't as big of a deal as everyone made it out to be. That it was optional. Like choosing whether to learn French or German in school. But deep down, I couldn't shake the fear that maybe I was wrong. Maybe love really was that magical, all-consuming force that made life worth living. And maybe I was just too broken to feel it. Or too stubborn to recognize it for what it was.

But in the end, I was still young.

Still just someone trying to figure out life before I could ever hope to understand what love was really all about.

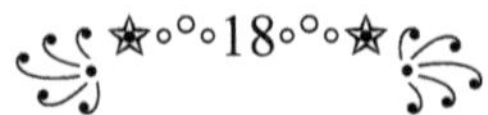

The Perception Of Fairytales

Once upon a time, bedtime stories made love seem simple. It was about a prince finding his princess. Those were the stories we grew up with. A love so perfect, so consuming, untouched by the weight of reality. And maybe that's why so many people spend their lives searching for it.

Some chase fairytale love because they're in love with the idea of love itself. The way it wraps around them like a warm embrace. The way it makes the world feel brighter, more meaningful. They don't just want love. They want the kind that feels like poetry. Like fate. They believe in soulmates, in destined meetings, in eyes locking across a crowded room and somehow just knowing. People who long for that kind of love live for the magic. For the serendipitous moments that make everything feel meant to be.

Others chase it because they see it as the highest, most sacred form of love. Proof that love can be something more. Something untouchable. Something beyond the ordinary. To them, love isn't just companionship. It's an all-consuming force. A reason to exist. Anything less feels empty. So, they hold onto that ideal. They chase it and refuse to settle for anything that doesn't set their soul on fire.

And then there are those who search for it because they've never truly known love. They've never felt the warmth of unconditional acceptance. Never experienced love without strings attached. That's why they long for a love that doesn't leave. That doesn't waver. That doesn't shatter under the weight of hardship or misunderstanding. They search for the kind of love that promises forever. Not just because they want it, but because they need it to exist. Because without it, love feels too uncertain. Too fragile.

The reason people chase fairytale love is because it promises something reality often cannot. Something bigger than the ordinary.

It offers certainty.

It offers passion.

It offers eternity.

And even when we know it might not be real. Even after we've seen the cracks in the stories. Even once we've learned that love is messier, more complicated, and sometimes more painful than the fairy tales ever told us. We still find ourselves searching for that magical kind of love.

Because deep down, we are all just looking for something that makes the world feel a little less harsh, and a little more beautiful.

As kids, we clung to every word of the fairytales we were told, our eyes wide with wonder, refusing to close until we heard them one more time. And so, even when we knew they would always end the same way, with a promise, a forever, a happily-ever-after, we were still in awe. Back then, we perceived love as an already known language, woven into every story, every song, every lesson passed down to us.

And so, we grew up chasing those same stories, believing we could mold love into the perfect story, just as perfect, just as timeless. But when it came time to write our own story, we found that love does not always follow the script we imagined. Some endings unravel, some take turns we never foresaw, and some aren't endings, just echoes of what could have been.

Part Two

When Love Destroys

Love Which Can't Be Defined As Cosmos

Elen had always believed in love. In the one and only. And by the time we were in high school, she finally found her so-called one. She had found her picture-perfect romance. When she met her Prince Charming in our first year, she truly believed she had stepped into the fairytale she had been waiting for her whole life. At first, it seemed like everything she wanted. He was charming in that effortless bad boy way, hitting her with sweet smiles, corny jokes, and just enough rebellion to make him interesting. They were inseparable from the start, like they had been pulled together by the same cosmic forces she had believed in since childhood. I remember how her eyes lit up when she talked about him, how she would tell me all the little things he did that made her feel like the center of the world. And for a while, it really did seem like she had found exactly what she had always dreamed of.

But it wasn't long before the cracks started to show.

Their relationship wasn't the whirlwind romance she had imagined. It was more like a storm. Beautiful and chaotic, always leaving a trace of destruction behind. They argued constantly, caught in a cycle of good days and bad ones that left them both exhausted. One day, they would be holding hands, whispering sweet nothings, posting couple selfies on Instagram. The next, she would be sitting beside me at lunch, picking at her food and pretending she wasn't wiping tears from her cheeks. *"They don't tell you about this part in the fairytales,"* she said once, her voice rough from the night before, when she had cried herself to sleep.

I tried to tell her that it was okay to let go, that not every love story was meant to last forever. But Elen couldn't let it go. She clung to the idea of what they could be. She clung to the love she thought they were supposed to have. *"We just need to work harder. I just need to work harder,"* she would say. *"All good relationships take hard work."*

But for them, it wasn't just hard work. It was war. And it was taking its toll on her.

The hard truth was that they brought out the worst in each other. Her jealousy made her feel like she was walking on eggshells every single day. She was constantly afraid of saying or doing anything wrong because she believed he would leave if she did. Her insecurities turned every disagreement into a catastrophe, and every missed step became proof that she wasn't good enough to be in a relationship. They were like fire and gasoline, igniting each other every time they came too close.

Even so, it wasn't long before she stopped talking to me altogether, because he mattered more.

Elen always knew what to do when things started to fall apart. She pulled away. At first, it was subtle. She canceled our plans, took longer to reply to my messages. But eventually, it was like she disappeared completely. She spent all her time with him, caught in that same cycle of fighting and making up, just like my parents used to when I was little. I tried reaching out, but it felt like shouting into a void.

One of the last times we spoke, she brushed me off with a tired smile and said, *"I'm fine."* But her voice wavered, and I knew she wasn't. I always knew.

Then one day, she was just gone. She had chosen him. Chosen *"love."*

We stopped seeing each other at school. Funny, because we always had classes near each other. But even then, she stopped looking at me. It was like she had erased herself from my life, and all I could do was watch from a distance as she disappeared into the deep waters of love.
Some weeks later, she showed up at my doorstep.
I welcomed her with open arms. She told me they had finally broken up. But by then, the damage had already been done. The spark in her eyes had faded, and the weight she carried had settled deep into her. She had poured so much of herself into that relationship, clinging to something that was never meant to last, that by the time it ended, there wasn't much of her left.

And as for us, we never truly found our way back to each other.
I don't know if it was because she was embarrassed, or because she couldn't face the reminders of who she used to be. Maybe it was easier for her to start over somewhere else, to leave behind the version of herself she had been when we were still friends.
But I still think about her. About the way she used to light up when she talked about her dreams. About the way she believed in love, like it was the answer to everything.

I hope she finds her way back to that version of herself someday.

Because if anyone deserves a real fairytale, it's Elen.

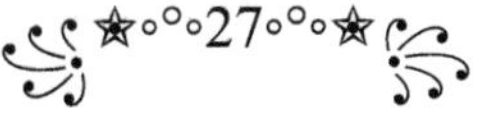

She loved the idea of love. She loved the joy it brought, the way it made her feel alive. But somewhere along the way, she forgot to love herself. She became so focused on earning the love of others that she lost sight of how important it was to love and care for herself first.

A Flower She Was, Withered She Became

There was once a girl I knew, someone whose heart seemed to beat with a rhythm all its own. Her name was Rosa, and from the moment I met her, I could tell that love meant something different to her. She longed for it in a way most people couldn't quite understand. But it wasn't the kind of love people usually talked about. Rosa wanted a love that was pure, simple, and free of conditions. A love that didn't demand, didn't wound, and didn't make her feel like she had to lose parts of herself to keep it. She craved a love that was effortless and unburdened. One that flowed freely without expectation, without pain.

But love wouldn't be that kind to her. And I would witness, firsthand, the lowest point of her search for it.

One evening she took me with her somewhere, though I had no idea where we were going at first. I just knew she needed me there. We walked in silence through the dimly lit streets, and before I knew it, we arrived at an empty kindergarten. The place was quiet, the glow of streetlights barely illuminating the small swings and slides that stood still in the night breeze. It was a place meant for children's laughter, for innocence. But that night, it was a place of heartbreak. Rosa walked ahead of me, and then I saw him. The guy she called her boyfriend. The one she had loved for so many years. He stood there, tall and unmoving, his arms crossed over his chest, his expression unreadable. And then, before I could understand what was happening, Rosa fell to her knees. Right there, in the dirt, she knelt before him, her hands clutching at his pants, her entire body trembling. She looked like a withered flower slowly falling apart.

"I'm sorry," she gasped between sobs. *"Please… just give me another chance. Please, I'll do anything. I can fix it. I promise, I can fix us."* Her voice was barely more than a whisper, cracking under the weight of her desperation. Tears streamed down her face, mixing with the dirt beneath her. Snot clung to her upper lip, and she didn't even try to wipe it away. She was beyond caring, beyond pride, beyond anything but the aching need for him to stay. For him to see her. To accept her again.
But he didn't move. He didn't reach for her. He didn't lift her up. Instead, he looked down at her with an expression that made my stomach turn.

Amusement.

He smirked, as if the sight of her, this girl who once spoke about love as something soft and beautiful, was nothing more than entertainment to him. As if she were a character in some tragic comedy, and he was the audience, watching with cold curiosity.
I wanted to scream at her to get up. To stop humiliating herself. To see what I was seeing. But she couldn't. She was blind to everything but him. To her, he was still Prince Charming. To him, she was a jester, nothing more than a joke.

He let out a small laugh, shaking his head as she sobbed harder.
"You're pathetic," he said, his voice sharp with cruelty. *"You think crying like this will change anything?"*
She sniffled, trying to catch her breath, her fingers tightening around the fabric of his jeans. *"I just love you,"* she whispered, her voice barely audible. Each word trembled.
"I don't know what I am without you."

And in that moment, I realized just how lost she had become. There was a vacancy in her eyes, a quiet absence I recognized too well. I had once worn it myself.

She wasn't begging for love anymore. She was begging for identity. For a reason to exist. She had given so much of herself away to him that she no longer knew how to stand on her own. Her self-worth had been chipped away piece by piece, and now she was trying to rebuild it by clinging to someone who could never make her whole again. But he didn't offer a hand. He didn't soften his gaze. Instead, he took a step back, forcing her grip to slip from him. He let her fall forward, her hands sinking into the dirt as if she belonged there, on her knees, crawling at his feet.

"Get up," he said. But there was no kindness in his voice. Just disgust. *"I don't want you anymore."* For a moment, she didn't move. Maybe she didn't even hear him. And then, after what felt like forever, she slowly pushed herself up. She didn't look at me, but I saw it in her face. She looked empty. Hollow. The realization that the love she believed in had never been real settled into her bones. She had spent so long searching for a love that wouldn't hurt her, but somewhere along the way, she began to mistake suffering for devotion. She believed that if she just gave enough, if she sacrificed enough, she could make it pure.

I wanted to take her hand. To pull her back from the edge. To remind her of how she used to speak about love. How she once believed in something softer, something better.

But that night, Rosa wasn't ready to hear it.

And so, we walked away from that empty kindergarten. Her footsteps were heavy, her body hunched beneath the weight of pain no one should carry alone. I stayed beside her, silent.

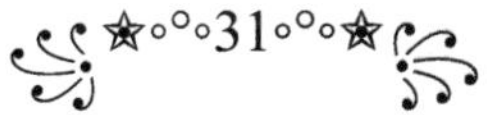

Because sometimes, love isn't about grand gestures or perfect endings. Sometimes, love is simply being there, quietly, while someone gathers the pieces of their own heart.

But weeks later, despite everything, despite the way he had treated her like nothing, he took her back. And she went to him.
I didn't believe it was love. It never felt like love.
It felt like something else. Something heavy and unhealthy. Something she couldn't seem to break free from, no matter how much it hurt her. And I knew, deep down, that he didn't take her back because he had finally seen her worth. He took her back because he knew she would always come when he called. That was his power over her. Familiarity dressed as love.

And all I did, all I could do, was stand by her. Watching. Hoping that one day, she would see what I saw. That one day, she would choose herself over the comfort of being chosen by someone who never truly saw her. Because sometimes love doesn't look like flowers or soft words. Sometimes, it's simply sitting beside someone in silence. Just being there, until they remember how to find their way back to themselves.

There are stories we inherit
not through blood,
but through silence.
Through the way a door closes,
through the pause before someone says,
"it was different back then."
I was born between
the apology that never came
and the forgiveness that was never asked for.
My mother taught me
how to stay too long.
My father taught me
how to love without touching the ground.
Both of them,
masters of endurance,
slaves to the myth
that love means holding on
even when the rope cuts deep.

Hand in Hand, Despite It All

My dad was a little taller than my mom, just a little more than eight and a half inches. She was barely five feet, and he stood at five foot eight. A Romanian small-town girl and a Serbian soldier on leave. They met in December 1990, when she was working part-time in a restaurant in the city. A long way from home. He and his friends would come in to eat and drink during military breaks, and somehow, between serving tables and stolen glances, something sparked between them.

By 1991, she was pregnant with my brother. Love had already spoken, and she followed it. She was drawn in, even though it meant losing everything else. Her parents were strict, religious, and unwilling to accept the life she had chosen. In their world, love was never a reason to go against tradition or to build a future with a man they didn't trust. So she was cast out, left with no home to return to. She stayed with him, hoping love would be enough to save them both. But love alone cannot feed a child. My parents were young and broke, unprepared for the weight of real life. My father still lived as if he had no responsibilities. He was restless, reckless, and distracted by his own desires. Mistresses came and went. His freedom remained untouched while my mother scraped together what she could to keep them alive. She stood for hours in the cold at the market, selling what little she had, trying to make enough for food and electricity.

My father's parents didn't make it any easier. They didn't help. Instead, they reminded her every day that she wasn't enough. A Romanian girl in a Serbian family. An outsider. A mistake. They belittled her, made her feel small, made sure she knew she didn't belong.

Through all of it, she stayed. She fought. Maybe because she had nowhere else to go. Maybe because she still believed in something better. She had always looked at life through rose-colored glasses. Fifteen years after my brother was born, I came into the world. Fifteen years of holding it together. Fifteen years of betrayal, survival, and the kind of love that begins as hope and ends as habit. Something in her finally broke. Maybe it was the exhaustion of loving someone who never truly loved her the way she needed. Maybe it was the realization that she could no longer live like that. She left.

She didn't just leave my father. She left the entire life she had built with him. She left the country, alone, in search of something steadier. Something that would let her breathe. She worked herself to the bone. Thin as she already was, she saved every cent and pushed forward, hoping to build something real. But even far from home, the dream never fully arrived. She had lost too much. Her parents. Her home. Her youth. Her hope. Her happiness. All she had left was a man she no longer recognized.

But my parents had a pattern. They would separate and find their way back to each other, only to break again. It was a cycle. A silent war between what had once been love and what had become necessity.

To make it worse, my mother also lost her son. Not to death, but to a world she could not understand. The boy she had sacrificed everything for fell into something dark. He lost himself in a life that had no place for faith, for family, or for love. And she watched him disappear from a distance, unable to pull him back. So she turned to the only things she could hold. Her work. Her prayers.

My father, meanwhile, threw himself into status and reputation. He wanted to be seen as a man of power. A man who mattered. His world was built on appearances. Where my mother's world was built on silence. And I was there in the middle of it all. Between them. Between their fights and reconciliations. Between my mother's pleading and my father's ambition. Between a house that never felt like home and a family that never quite fit together.

Even so, I saw their love. I saw it in tiny moments, in the shadows. I took the crumbs and convinced myself they meant something. Even if that love left scars.

After my mother left, after we caught him with another woman, he came crawling back. And she took him in. With tears on her face and swollen eyes from crying, she let him in because she loved him. Because she had only ever loved him. And in his own way, he loved her too. He lived for her. But his mind was troubled. He could never hold still long enough to treat her the way she deserved.
Still, sometimes, he kissed her. And for a moment, she let herself believe. A flicker of something old would stir inside her. Like smelling a perfume from another lifetime and remembering who you used to be. But she wasn't that girl anymore. The one who gave up everything for love.

She could never go back.

That kind of love had cost her too much. Even when the kiss moved something inside her, she knew it was just a ghost. A memory. A past too distant to return to.

Now, when I look at my father, I see a man who has aged. A man who has changed, not out of reflection, but out of exhaustion. Life wore him down. He has settled. He has become still. He has chosen my mother, not with passion or apology, but with presence. He sits beside her each night. They share space. They exist quietly together. This is not the love they once had. It does not burn. It does not steal breath or spark longing. It is a love made of routine. Of history. Of staying. Not the love of stolen glances in a restaurant, but the kind that remains because nothing else survived.

Because after everything, after all the leaving, the breaking, the returning, what else was there but to stay? What else was there but to follow the rhythm of time? The rules of age. The rules of endurance. The rules of dying beside the person you once chose. Right or wrong, it was still love.

And now, when I see them, I see myself. I see how their story is woven into my bones. How their choices echo in the way I understand love. I do not hold anger for how they loved me, or how they loved each other.
But it shaped me.

To me, love has never meant softness. It has never meant passion. It has meant survival.

I grew up in the ruins of their love. And I still stand in it. It is not whole, but not completely broken either. It is not entirely a tragedy, but it is far from a fairytale. It is something fragile. Something real. And somehow, despite everything, it is still standing.

Maybe that is why, as I grew older, I kept reaching for any kind of connection. Longing for love in any form. Longing for someone, anyone, to choose me back.

Dear Mother, Dear Father,
I grew up in the house your love built. Not one of brick or stone, but one made of glances, long silences, and the sound of things left unsaid. You stayed, not always with each other, but near enough to hurt, and far enough to miss.

Mother, you taught me how to endure. You gave and gave until there was nothing left. I saw it in your eyes when you thought no one was watching. I heard it in the way you spoke to God like He was the only one who ever truly listened. You were the soft armor of our home, always holding it together with your silence and hope.

Father, you loved in ways I didn't always understand. Quietly. From a distance. I used to think you weren't trying, but now I think maybe you just didn't know how. Maybe no one ever showed you what gentle love looked like. Still, I saw it sometimes, in the way you lingered in doorways, in the way you fixed things without being asked, in the way you always came back.

I know you love me. I know you always did.
And I love you, too. Not perfectly. But deeply.

I carry you both with me. In the way I walk through the world, in the way I love and lose and try again. I carry your pain, your strength, your hope. I carry the echo of your mistakes and the quiet resilience behind your survival. And I forgive you. For the things that hurt, and for the things you couldn't change. I forgive you, because in your own ways, you never stopped loving me.

With all my heart,
and all the pieces you left in me,
Your child.

The Cost of Belonging

For years, I was captivated by the idea of longing. Not for something specific, and not for love the way others spoke about it. I didn't long for the kind of love you see in movies or read about in fairytales. I longed for the feeling of wanting itself. The ache of reaching for something just out of sight. I yearned for acceptance. A place where I fit. Maybe I longed for a person who would look at me and say, *you, just as you are, are enough.*

And so, whenever I found myself in a group of people, I longed to be truly seen. And even when I was alone, I longed for someone who could make me feel less invisible. That longing became a quiet restlessness. It wove its way through my life, blurring the lines between what was real and what was only the reflection of my own desperate desire.

I never truly understood love. What I saw growing up wasn't love. It was what my parents called love, and it was dark. Their version was strained by unspoken pain and quiet endurance. Their love taught me that love was something to survive, not something to celebrate. And because of that, I came to see love not as a safe haven, but as a battlefield where people lost themselves trying to hold on.

The truth is, I never wanted to look back and question what love actually meant. I was never taught to question it. Not in school, not in life. But the thought still found me, again and again. And each time it did, it never came with warmth. My reflections on love were rarely kind. They carried more fear than hope, more doubt than desire. Love always felt like something meant for others, not for me. In school, we were taught equations, grammar, and history, but never the language of love. Never the emotion that quietly shapes our lives, that defines so much of our joy and sorrow. We learned nothing about it. Nothing about how it builds us or breaks us. When it comes to love, people are expected to dive in without ever being taught how to swim. And so, I was left to figure it out on my own, with nothing but the fragments I had seen and the ache I carried with me. I overanalyzed everything. Every word. Every gesture. Because I didn't know what love was or what it was supposed to mean.

But then I met her.
She slipped into my life as quietly and effortlessly as a phone notification. A simple moment that changed everything. She was like a ray of sunshine, speaking in a dialect I hadn't learned yet. She made me laugh. She made me feel like me. For the first time in my life, I felt alive and appreciated.
But something felt wrong. Or maybe, not wrong exactly. Confusing. Was this how love was supposed to feel? Maybe. Yes. I didn't know. Now I realize that it wasn't love, not the same kind people talk about. But still, I liked her. She was a girl, and I liked her. That alone felt like a quiet rebellion. The truth behind it was that it wasn't the feeling that scared me. It wasn't the fact that she was a girl. That didn't matter to me. What mattered was the thought of my parents finding out. How would they look at me? What would they say? Liking her meant going against everything I'd been taught. Every unspoken rule. Every expectation. It felt like choosing between who I was and who I was supposed to be.

After a year of being with her, not officially, but emotionally, I still hadn't accepted myself. I couldn't. Every time my parents asked about this special "friend," I couldn't meet their eyes. If they knew the truth, if they knew how I really felt, I was certain they'd see me as broken. A virus. An outcast. Someone who had strayed too far from the path they believed God would bless.

So, I got scared. I told her it was me. I pulled the classic move and claimed I was the problem. Maybe I was. I pushed her away, thinking it would somehow protect us both. As if breaking my own heart was better than letting her get hurt.

After her, I was sure I was unlovable. Undeserving. That even love itself had given up on me. So, I let her go. And I convinced myself again that love was never meant for me.

Years later, everyone around me seemed to be discovering their own definitions of love. And suddenly, I was expected to do the same. But I had no love. Not even a trace left inside me. It had been taken before I ever understood what it meant to love and be loved.
Then I saw him. Not in a fairytale way. More like a shadow. He wasn't light, and neither was I. But for a moment, it felt like maybe, just maybe, we could be something in between.

"Hi," he said.

"Hello," I said.

And that was it. Two words. And something shifted. My friends, full of excitement, started pushing him toward me. I didn't know what to do. He scared me, yet I didn't stop him.

I started collecting pieces of him. Like girls in middle school did when they had crushes. I mimicked them. I noticed the way his mossy green eyes darkened when he squinted, a change that only happened when he smiled. But there was nothing warm in that smile. It wasn't kind. It was the kind of smile that made your skin crawl. A smile worn like a mask. A smile which crawled under my skin. It lodged itself in my mind, spreading slowly like poison. It wrapped itself around my thoughts, and no matter how I tried, I couldn't shake it loose.

From the beginning, I knew something wasn't right. But I told myself this was normal. That this was what love looked like. Love, as I had come to know it, had always been twisted.
So I stayed. I went along with it. I pretended it was fine, even when it wasn't. Even when the way he looked at me felt wrong. Not like someone being seen, but like something being owned. Like I was his to keep, not his to love.
And slowly, I became someone I didn't recognize. Someone who stayed silent. Someone who accepted what never should have been accepted. With time I started to miss my room. My iPad. My quiet dreams. I missed not pretending.

Eventually, I left.

I picked myself up. I saw myself again. I walked away, like my mother once did. But unlike her, I never looked back. Not at him. Not at the version of love I had told myself was enough.
Because it wasn't love. None of it was.
One moment felt like connection. The next felt like regret. I had spent years mistaking something else for love. Letting it excuse how others treated me. I drifted from the values I was raised with. From my own boundaries. I told myself love was supposed to hurt. That being used was the price of being wanted.

I accepted scraps and called them blessings. I kept reshaping myself into what others needed, hoping that would finally make me enough. But the truth is, the problem was never love.
The problem was how I saw love. Through a lens clouded by the belief that I didn't deserve more.

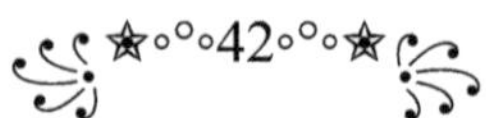

Through watching love and trying to experience it myself, I realized that people are always asking questions about it. Even when they don't say them out loud. And no matter how different those questions sound, they always return to the same quiet ache.
How do we find love?
How does it feel when it's real?
How do we hold on to it?
And how do we survive when it breaks us?

But for me, the question has always sounded different.
How do I even learn to love when I never truly knew what it was to begin with?
And more importantly,
how do I teach myself that I'm worthy of it?

The Undoing

I left pieces of myself
in the way I said yes
when I meant maybe,
in the way I stayed
when I wanted to leave.
Love didn't take me all at once.
It took me in teaspoons.
A laugh.
A silence.
A name I stopped using.
By the time I looked back,
I wasn't there.

The Lack Of Self Love

Some people spend their lives searching for love, believing that the right person will fix everything, fill the emptiness, and make them feel whole. They hold onto the idea that love is the answer to everything. That a fairytale romance will be the missing piece they have been longing for. But in chasing that dream, they often miss the most important part. Learning to love themselves first.
With every passing moment, they pour their hearts into relationships that were never meant to last, investing more in the potential of what could be than accepting what actually is. They give everything they have, hoping that someone else's love will fill the spaces inside them that feel incomplete. The space they cannot seem to love for themselves. But the more they give, the more they lose themselves, until eventually, they are left feeling empty. Left wondering why love always slips through their fingers. Wondering if they are the problem.

It is true that love from another person can be beautiful. But it is fleeting when there is no foundation of self-worth beneath it. No amount of affection from someone else can truly heal the wounds that come from not loving yourself. And yet, it is easy to keep searching for validation in another person, hoping they will be the cure.

The problem lies in how many people do not realize that the missing piece is not someone else. They overlook the idea that it might be self-love. You cannot pour from an empty cup. To truly care for others, you must first care for yourself. If you have not taken the time to nurture and complete who you are, you cannot expect someone else to do it for you.

The journey toward self-love is not easy. It often comes with heartbreak and painful realizations. But the greatest love story is the one where they finally learn to love themselves first. Only then can they truly experience the deep, fulfilling love they have always dreamed of. Not because of someone else, but because they already hold it within.

And so, I hope that those who have seen themselves in Elen, in Rosa, or in anyone who has ever lost themselves in the name of love, and those who might recognize something of themselves in who I once was, the one who stayed quiet, who bent and broke just to feel wanted will one day find their way back to themselves.
If this is you, if you see yourself in any of these people, I hope you come to understand that love is not something you have to earn by sacrificing who you are. It is not meant to be a reflection of someone else's approval.

Real love begins within you. It grows when you choose yourself.
Not because someone else finally did, but because you did.
Nothing shines brighter than a person who knows their worth. Who has learned to love themselves fully, gently, and without condition.
You are not too much.
You are allowed to take up space.
You are allowed to heal.
You are allowed to walk away.
And maybe, in time, you will come to see what I see now.
That love does not have to hurt to be real.

Dear Things, I fear,
You haunt me in way too many ways. You creep into my thoughts when I least expect it, curling around my mind like smoke, impossible to grasp but always there.

I fear **dying**, not just because I don't know what comes after, but because I fear leaving too soon, before I've loved enough, lived enough, been enough.

I fear **losing my beloved things**, not because they are just objects, but because they hold pieces of me, memories, moments, parts of a past I can never get back if they slip away.

I fear **not understanding what people say**, of being lost in translation, left behind, not knowing the right words to make myself belong.

I fear **not enjoying my life**, of it slipping through my fingers while I watch from the sidelines, waiting for something to change, waiting for something to feel right.

I fear **never finding anyone who loves me**, of being too much or not enough, of always reaching but never holding, of searching for home in people who never stay.

I Really hope I find someone who feels like home, who makes me feel like I truly belong.

Yours always,
Me.

Part Three

The Learning

Even if I didn't find love in my childhood,
even if the people who should have given it never did,

I've learned it was never about me being unlovable.

I was just looking in the wrong places.

For so long, as a kid, as a teenager,
I thought love was something distant, unreal,
something I could never understand.
But now I know that was never true.

Love was always there.

I just had to stop searching for it where it didn't exist.

Passion, Obsession, and Tragedy

With time, I've come to accept that love is an enigma. Love is elusive, mysterious, and difficult to understand. It works like an invisible force, reshaping the way we see the world without us even realizing it.

For many, love begins as something distant. Sometimes it begins as something irrelevant. An abstract idea spoken of in books, glimpsed in movies, heard in songs, or observed in the lives of others. Some people dismiss love entirely, believing they are immune to its pull, convinced they can move through life untouched by its influence. But love has a way of slipping in unnoticed. It transforms indifference into curiosity, curiosity into longing, and longing into hunger. It begins as a lingering thought, a subtle shift in perspective, a yearning you can't quite explain. And then, suddenly, it consumes you. I've watched from a distance, observing how love quietly takes hold of others. But I've felt it too. It began slowly, almost invisibly, and then all at once, it was everything. I've seen how the world begins to orbit around its presence. Every moment becomes charged with meaning. Every day is touched by its shadow. Love rearranges your priorities, bends your logic, and redefines what once felt certain.

Love does not ask for permission. It weaves itself into everything until life before it feels muted, like a memory stripped of color.

In history the word "love" has always existed. It has been associated with deep affection and sacrifice. Over time, it evolved to represent everything from romantic passion to unconditional bonds. Across cultures, love has been the subject of mythology, philosophy, and art. A force so profound that entire belief systems have been built around its pursuit.

From the ancient Greeks distinguishing between eros, philia, and agape, to modern psychology dissecting attachment and emotional bonds, love has remained one of the most defining and studied human experiences.

Another moment in history that reshaped how love was perceived occurred during the Renaissance. In that era, love was no longer confined to duty, tradition, or arranged partnership. It became a subject of longing, admiration, and artistic celebration. Love was reimagined as an ideal that blended passion with intellect, emotion with inspiration. The Renaissance embraced the ideals of courtly love and romantic devotion. Love became something that could ignite beauty, something that could elevate the human soul. Shakespeare's works, like *Romeo and Juliet* and *Othello*, captured love in its most intense forms, portraying it as divine and transcendent, but also as a force capable of destruction. Poets wrote sonnets that turned longing into art. Painters like Botticelli portrayed love as ethereal, transformative, and sometimes tormenting.
This era solidified the idea that love was not just an emotion. It became an obsession. An ideal to chase. A force strong enough to define a person's entire existence.

When love is at its highest, it becomes a kind of madness. It dictates thoughts, decisions, and movements. It is intoxicating. It blinds as much as it illuminates. It is what makes hearts race and hands tremble. It is the reason people stay. The reason they fight, sacrifice, and surrender. When love is present, it feels eternal.

But what happens when love is lost?

Love, when taken away, does not simply vanish. It leaves a void. An absence that feels unbearable. The world grows dull, quieter, and emptier. The intensity that once fueled passion transforms into longing, regret, or bitterness. It reshapes the one who remains, leaving them to wonder if love was ever truly theirs.
But if you look at it rationally, love isn't just about having or losing. It is about transformation. Even when it disappears, it leaves something behind. Love lingers in memories, in scars, in the lessons we carry forward. It changes us. It never leaves us untouched. And maybe that is its true power. Not just in its presence, but in the way it forever alters those who have felt its touch. There is something quietly beautiful about that.

Through observation, I've witnessed love in many forms. In the way people hold each other. In the way they speak, the way they suffer, the way they rejoice. Love is not just something you experience firsthand. It reveals itself in the quiet moments between people. In the sacrifices made, in the longing glances, in the whispered words. Whether we embrace it or resist it, love shapes us. It leaves behind a story that continues even after it is gone.

But when love becomes tragic, it reflects something darker. A side of human nature that twists and breaks what was once soft. It shows how love, when fueled by insecurity or control, can lead to ruin instead of redemption. In these stories, love becomes a fire that consumes. Devotion becomes destruction. The tragedy of love isn't that it exists, but that sometimes it cannot survive in a world that is too chaotic, too unforgiving, or too divided.

Over the years, love became a puzzle I could never piece together. I saw it in ways that felt tangled, unclear, and distant from the fairytales everyone else seemed to believe in. It was never simple.

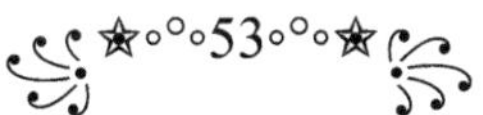

Never perfect. I spent years searching for something real, something I could hold. But it always felt just out of reach. I kept lingering, but nothing stayed.

It wasn't until years later, once I had changed, once I had matured, that I could finally look back and recognize a special form of love that had always been there.

The purest and most unconditional love I have ever known came from Tory.

A Heart Once Bright, Now Faded

There was once a woman named Tory, whose heart radiated warmth and tenderness, a quiet light in the lives of everyone lucky enough to know her. I met her when I was just a small child, newly arrived in a country where I knew no one. It was a meeting born of coincidence, the kind that alters the course of a life without anyone realizing it in the moment.

Our faucet had broken, and water flooded into the apartment below her apartment. My parents, worried and deeply apologetic, brought me along when they went downstairs to speak with her. I couldn't have known it then, but that was the beginning of a bond that would grow into something as deep as family. A love that felt familiar, as if it had always existed.

From that day on, Tory became a constant presence in my life. She became my protector, always there when my parents couldn't be. My childhood, often filled with long, lonely hours while they were away, grew brighter because of her.

She was a small, fragile woman, her body prone to injury, yet she carried a strength in her heart that made everything she did feel larger than life. Despite her frailty, she always showed up for me. Not through grand gestures, but in the small things. In her patience. In her quiet, unwavering kindness. She gave me a kind of love I didn't truly understand until years later, when I began to grasp what love really meant.

When I think back to her home, I remember it always being filled with life even in its quietest moments. She was the most creative woman I knew, able to turn simple objects into beautiful works of art. I would often sit at the small table in her living room, watching her work on her latest project, mesmerized by how she brought beauty out of nothing.

She had a collection of delicate porcelain figurines and little treasures, each one seeming to hold a piece of the world inside it. I remember once, without thinking, I took one. A tiny figure with a delicate shine. I expected her to be upset when I returned it, but she simply smiled. She told me I could keep it a little longer, that it was okay, and that I could bring it back when I was ready. There was no scolding. No disappointment. Only an understanding that didn't need words. That was how she loved me. Unconditionally. Without judgment. But back then, I didn't understand why she was always so kind to me. Why she wanted me by her side. I couldn't grasp the depth of her care. It was as if she saw something in me that I couldn't see in myself, something worth protecting. Worth loving. She showed me love, but not the kind I had known before. The love I was familiar with was jagged and unpredictable. It came from need, from duty, from expectation. Never from the simple desire to give. To nurture. To be there. The love I knew had strings. It was never soft.

Tory's love was something different. Something I would only begin to understand much later.

Her love was quiet and uncomplicated, free of conditions or expectations. It lingered softly in a room, offering comfort without asking for anything in return. She loved me not out of obligation, not because she had to, but because she simply did. Fully, gently, and with her whole heart.

For a long time, I couldn't see it for what it was. I didn't have the words to name it. I didn't have the understanding to receive it. I had grown up believing that love had to be earned, measured, and repaid. I didn't yet know that love could simply exist. That it could just be, it could be steady, patient, and unconditional.

The way Tory gave it to me, as naturally as breathing.

Her love lived in the little things. When I felt especially alone, she would invite me to her apartment for one of her little *"events,"* hosting me with care, as if I were the most important guest in the world. Even as she grew older and more fragile, she never stopped opening her door. And when the stairs became too much, she found other ways to reach me. Handwritten notes in my mailbox. Tiny gifts. Trinkets. Cards with soft words tucked inside.

Each one was a quiet reminder that I was never truly alone.

She once told me a story from her youth. How she came to understand love. She had fallen for a man in the kind of way that softens the world around you. Their love wasn't loud, but it was steady. Woven into the quiet moments. The way he held her hand. The way his eyes found hers in a room full of people. She told me love wasn't about declarations or dramatic passion. It was about presence. About trust. About feeling like you've come home. Even after he passed, she carried him with her. She never loved anyone the same way again. She didn't need to. Her heart had chosen him, and it stayed his. Quietly. Faithfully. For the rest of her life.

I thought about how I've let love treat me. How I've seen it treat others. How often it came wrapped in confusion, in expectation, in hurt. I thought about the younger version of me. The one who bent and twisted to be loved. The one who mistook attention for affection.

And then I thought of her.

Even if I hadn't fully understood it then, something about Tory stayed with me. Her way of loving became a soft echo in my life. The kind you don't recognize until much later. And without even realizing it, she taught me how to love that way too.

To love with patience.
To love with constancy.
To love without condition.

Even if it took years for me to see it, her way of loving became mine. I wanted to thank her. To tell her I understood. To tell her she had shaped me.

But when I went to visit, Tory was gone.

I hadn't seen her in a long time, even though I'd promised myself I would. I kept saying I'd go soon. That there would be more time. But I let life get in the way. I disappeared into a difficult chapter. I disappeared from her life too.

I hadn't realized how much time had passed until I stood in front of her apartment again. I hadn't planned it. Something inside me just told me to go. To return to the place that once felt like home.

I knocked softly. Then again, a little louder.

Nothing.

I waited longer than I needed to. The silence on the other side felt heavier than I expected. When I walked inside, it hit me all at once.

The apartment was empty.
The scent of her. The soft hum of her life. Gone. The trinkets, the figurines, the warmth, there was no longer anything there.
It felt as if she had never been there at all.

My heart sank. I knew what had happened before I asked anyone.
Tory had passed away. Quietly. Peacefully. Without making a sound. And I wasn't there to say goodbye.
The guilt was unbearable. I had promised her I would visit. That I wouldn't let time slip away. But I failed her. I had been so caught in my pain that I neglected the one person who had always been there for me. The one who loved me even when I didn't know how to love myself.

Now, all I have are memories. Her arms when I was small. Her handwritten notes. Her soft voice and unwavering presence.
And even though I let her down, I know Tory would forgive me. She always forgave me.

Looking back now, I realize that Tory's love, the love she learned from her husband, was something that transcended time. She passed it on to me, and I now carry it forward. I give it to others in the way she once gave it to me.

Her love changed my life.
And it will live on in the way I love now.
Patient.
Steady.
Always enough.

My dearest Tory,
I've finally taken the initiative to write to you. I know you know how much I miss you, but I want you to know that I've put your letters up on my wall. It's my special memory wall, a wall of things I love, and each letter from you is a piece of my heart.

I love you now, in a way I never understood before. I've learned what love really is because of you, I've learned that it's simple, kind, and always there, just like you were. I keep your letters close, and every time I look at them, I feel your love wrapping around me, like a warm hug. Thank you for always loving me so purely, even when I didn't know how to love myself. You'll always have a special place in my heart.

With all my love,
I miss you.

Growth In The Eyes Of Love

I watched her grow before she ever noticed me.

At first, she feared me. Not because I had hurt her, but because of what others had done in my name. She saw me twisted into promises that fell apart, spoken through clenched jaws and quiet tears. She heard me shouted, weaponized, withheld.

She learned early that I was something loud, something fleeting, something heavy, something earned.

Something she wasn't worthy of.

When she was a child, I tried to reach her. In soft moments. In kind smiles. In the arms of a woman who gave without asking for anything in return. But the noise in her world was too loud, and she was too busy learning to survive.

In her youth, she chased me. Ran toward anything that looked like me. Anyone who mirrored back the ache she carried. She offered herself in fragments. I tried to whisper, to pull her gently away, but she mistook my silence for absence.

I watched her give herself to those who didn't know how to receive.

She thought I meant sacrifice. That I required her to shrink. She thought I would finally stay if she could just be enough. But she didn't understand me.

I waited.

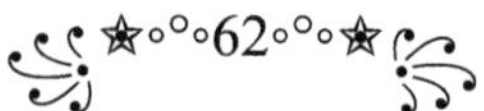

I watched her hurt.

And still, I stayed.

Still waiting for her.

Still hoping she would realize that she was worthy of me.

When she closed her heart, when she said she was done with me, I remained quietly beside her. I left notes in the kindness of strangers. I lived in the eyes of someone who listened without interrupting. I was there, in the hands that never asked her to become someone else.

I was always there.

I did not arrive all at once. I came to her in pieces. In lessons. In quiet unlearning. In the realization that I did not demand her suffering.

She began to notice me not in the grand, dramatic moments, but in the soft ones.

She began noticing my presence in the calm moments, the moments after the chaos.
In the steadiness of being understood.
In the comfort of not having to explain herself.

Slowly, she stopped begging for me.
Stopped proving.
Stopped chasing.

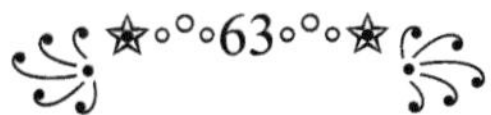

And that was when she finally found me.

Not in someone else. But within herself.

She learned that I am not the fire you burn for. I am the warmth you return to.

I am not a test.
I am not a reward.
I am not something to survive.

I am the space you breathe in when you are finally safe.

And after everything, she understands me now.

I never asked her to be perfect. I only ever asked her to be real.

And with time she learned what that meant. She realized that she is worthy.
She is lovable.
She deserves love.

Love isn't a map you follow, but a journey you stumble upon, and with him, I finally found the path I was meant to walk.

Love That Found Us

Love does not always arrive the way we expect it to. Sometimes, it lingers at the edges of our existence, waiting for the right moment to step forward and reveal itself. Other times, it crashes in like a sudden storm, shifting everything out of place before we even realize we've been caught in it.

For me, love was never something I believed would truly reach me, let alone change me. It was just an idea, something I longed to grasp, something I hoped to claim as my own. I saw it as a distant light, something others found, something I observed, but never something meant for me. Love had always felt like an illusion. Either forced upon you or stolen away before you ever had the chance to hold it. I watched it play out in the lives of others, quietly, from the sidelines.

Until I met *him.*

The one I would grow to love.

And suddenly, love was no longer distant. I was no longer an observer. Love was no longer just a word or an idea. Love was him. I met him in high school. At first, he was just another face in the crowd, someone moving through the hallways like everyone else. But something about him stood out. He was tall, standing at six-foot-one, with golden curls that framed his face like light. His eyes were the color of deep sapphires, shifting under sunlight like ocean tides.

There was quietness in him. A kind of confidence that didn't demand attention but quietly held it. He felt like the kind of person who was always halfway between staying and drifting away.

Unpredictable, like the sea itself. He didn't try to be noticed, but I noticed him every time.
And I was nothing like him.
I was smaller, just five-foot-two, with dark hair and shifting eyes that changed with the light. I had spent most of my life performing versions of myself just to feel like I fit in. While he had a way of seeing people, really seeing them, I had learned to disappear behind what others wanted me to be.

We were different in every way imaginable.

And yet, for reasons I couldn't explain, we kept glancing in each other's direction. It wasn't instant. We didn't fall into each other's arms. It wasn't dramatic. It was slow. A quiet pull. A soft unfolding. Like fate nudging us closer without either of us realizing why.
There were no grand confessions between us. No sweeping moments of revelation. Just a glance that lingered too long. A conversation that didn't need to continue, but neither of us wanted it to end. It was a series of moments that felt ordinary to the world, but to us, they were everything.

His presence didn't feel new. It felt like something I had always known. Like returning to a place I had never been, but somehow remembered. Like finding something I didn't know I was missing, and realizing I had been waiting for it all along.
Still, I tried to resist it. The aching pull in my chest. I tried to stay away.

But I couldn't.

There was always something, timing, coincidence, or maybe just the quiet persistence of two souls recognizing each other, that brought us back to the same place.

Back to the tension.
Back to the question.
Back to the space between almost and never.

Wanting and fearing.
Holding on and letting go.
Everything shifted in our second year of high school. But not in the way fairytales promise. There was no perfect moment. No magic. We found each other in the middle of chaos. In a time when neither of us was whole.

He carried his past quietly, with unspoken wounds. I carried mine like a shadow. We were two people still learning how to stand. Still learning how to breathe beneath everything we'd been through.
For so long, I believed love was something you had to earn. That it followed a path, a rulebook. That you had to prove you were worthy. But in the middle of the mess, when nothing else made sense, he did. He made sense. I don't even remember how it happened. One moment, we were just two people moving through life. The next, we were more. Not quite friends. Not quite lovers. Something in between. I remember sitting beside him once, silence stretching between us like a held breath. And then I whispered, without thinking, I said: *"I wish your light could shine into my world."*
I hadn't meant to say it. I hadn't even known I was thinking it. But once the words escaped, they were real. He was light. Not the obvious kind. Not the kind that blazed. But the kind that warmed quietly. The kind that makes the world feel just a little less heavy.

And I had lived so long in the dimness of fear. Fear of love. Fear of being seen.

But with him, love wasn't something to be feared.
With him, love was simple.

Falling in love with him wasn't one moment. It was a hundred small moments that wove themselves into something I couldn't deny. Maybe it was the way he looked at me like he truly saw me. Maybe it was the way his fingers brushed mine, hesitant, then steady. Maybe it was how silence between us never felt empty.

And in the end, he chose me.

He. Chose. Me.

In a world full of choices, he picked me.

We didn't rush anything. We let it unfold slowly. There were late nights filled with whispered confessions. Days spent learning every detail about each other, the kind of details most people overlook. Like how he fidgeted with his hands when he was nervous. Or how, when he slept, his lips parted slightly, forming the softest shape of a heart.

I had spent so long trying to force myself into the version of love my parents wanted for me. A love that was structured. Predictable. Based on duty, not desire. But with him, love didn't follow rules. It simply was. Because, in the end, it was his love that found me. The kind of love that isn't loud or urgent, but soft and steady. The kind of love that doesn't rush, doesn't demand, doesn't need to be chased. It just arrives. And stays.

He was my first real love. The first person I gave my whole heart to without needing to be anyone else but myself.

And maybe that's what love really is.
Not a plan. Not a fairytale. Not a rule to follow.

Just something that happens when you're finally ready to stop pretending. When you're finally ready to be seen.

And I found it.
I found *love*,
I found it with *him*.

The Beauty of Loving

Reasons to Open Your Heart

Because sometimes the world feels too big, and you feel too small. There are days when the weight of existence presses down on you, and all you want is for someone to pull you close, to remind you that you don't have to carry it all alone.

Because, in a sea of strangers, you'll long for a hand to hold, something steady when everything else feels uncertain. Someone who knows you well enough to find you in a crowded room, who reaches for you instinctively, without needing to ask.

Because there's something undeniably beautiful in the thought of someone choosing you every day, in all your moods, in all your mess. Not out of obligation, not out of habit, but because they simply want to.

Because love is in the small things: knowing how you drink your coffee, reminding you to take an umbrella when it rains, remembering the song that always makes you smile.

Because sometimes, just hearing someone say, *"You'll be okay"* makes it easier to believe.

Because there's something captivating about the way people look when they talk about something they're passionate about, the way their whole face lights up, their hands animated, their voices full of life. You'll want to be the one who gets to see that look often.

Because road trips are better with someone in the passenger seat, and long stretches of silence feel less empty when shared. Love isn't just in the big, dramatic moments, it's in the quiet moments of simply existing alongside each other.

There Was Before I Loved You, But Never an After

I. The Before

Before him, love was only something I observed from a distance.
It lived in the pages of the books I clung to, in the lyrics of songs that played softly through my headphones, in whispered conversations I overheard but never truly grasped.
It was everywhere, woven into the world around me like a language I could not speak, a door I had never dared to walk through.

I told myself I did not need it.
That I was whole on my own.
That love was just another thing people chased, not because they understood it, but because they were afraid to live without it.

But then, he knocked on my door.
And suddenly, love was no longer abstract or unreachable.
It stood before me in the shape of a boy with soft eyes and steady hands.

It was not a storm, crashing in to turn my world upside down.
It was a quiet shift, like the seasons changing when no one is paying attention.
Like the first warmth of spring after a winter I had not even realized had been so cold.

And for the first time, I understood.
Love was not about completing me.
It was about seeing myself more clearly through someone else's gentle gaze.
It was about freedom.

About coming home to myself and realizing I had never truly known what warmth was until then.

And I thought:
Love is truly beautiful.
And nothing compares to the peace it brings when it is soft, real, and kind.

II. The During

Loving him is like waking up in a room filled with morning light, the kind that spills gently across the floor and wraps itself around you without asking for anything in return.
It is soft and constant, never loud or demanding, just always there, like the sun rising even when you forget to look for it.

It is something I step into each day, a quiet invitation to begin again, to breathe a little easier, to notice the beauty in the smallest moments.
In the way he reaches for my hand without thinking.
In the way his smile curves slowly, like he is still surprised by how much he feels.
In the way his eyes find mine, even across a crowded room, like they are always looking for home.

I measure time by him now.
By the way his voice softens when he is tired.
By the rhythm of his breathing, steady and safe beside me.
By the way his laughter stays with me, echoing in my mind long after he is gone.

I wonder how I ever lived without this.
Without the way my name sounds when he says it, like a secret he keeps only for me.
Without the way his presence turns silence into something sacred, a kind of quiet that does not feel empty, but whole.
A quiet where I can simply be.

Without the feeling of us, stitched into everything.
In the gentle brush of a hand, the shared glance across the room, the unspoken understanding that this, whatever this is, is real.

This is love, in its purest form.
This is what it means to be truly seen, not just for who I am, but for who I am becoming beside him.

He is love.
Not the kind that burns fast and fades, but the kind that stays.
A love that is patient, kind, and full of grace.
A love that meets me where I am and still sees more.

In his eyes, I have found a home I never knew I was looking for.
A place where my heart settles with ease, where the chaos quiets.
And in his arms, I have found something even deeper than comfort.
I have found a warmth that reaches the parts of me I used to hide.
I have found a reason to not run anymore.

With him, love is not just a feeling.
It is a way of being.
And in that love, I have finally learned what it means to be truly held.

III. The After (Or The Fear of It)

You are still here.
I know this.
And yet,
There are moments when I feel the weight of a future I do not want.

A world where I wake up and reach for him, only to find emptiness.
A version of me that moves through the days without him beside me.
Where love is no longer a presence, but a memory I carry.
I do not know what that version of me looks like.
And I do not want to know.

So, I do not think about it.
I do not give it a name.
I do not look too closely at that quiet, aching fear.

Because there was a time before I loved him,
and now there is a time where I do.
And as long as I can, I will live here,
in this space where he still exists,
where love is not something I mourn, but something I hold.

There was a before I loved you,
but never an after.

Because love like this stays.
It does not vanish.
It softens, reshapes, and settles into the bones of who I am.
It does not disappear.
It simply becomes something new.

And for you,
for your love,
for the way it changed me,
I will always be grateful.

I love you.

And then,
it was all about you.
Songs I knew by heart
began to remind me of you.
They weren't just songs,
they were the sound of missing you.
My words turned into mirrors,
each one catching your light and reflecting it.
I even wrote like a poet undone,
finding you in everything,
you became a breath of fresh air,
a drop of rain,
a quiet moment.
With you,
I wrote a fairytale,
not of crowns,
but of becoming.
But of rising.
Of love that feels like home.
With you,
love became timeless.
It became our forever after.

Part Fours

My Words full of Love

The Soft Glow Of Warmth

If anyone were to ask me about love today,
I'd tell them about you.

I'd speak of the way your ocean eyes gaze into mine,
How your smile pulls gentle lines beneath your eyes,
And how, when I share things that spark my interest,
A quiet and wide smile blooms on your face.

I'd tell them how it feels to be cared for,
How love wraps itself around you like a warm embrace,
How it stirs a fuzzy warmth inside,
And how, in your presence, it feels effortless.

I'd say love is worth the experience,
That there's no such thing as being beyond its reach,
No such thing as "unlovable."
For no one is beyond love,
And everyone deserves it.

And how love feels like a summer day that lingers,
The kind where the sun hangs low, and full of promise.
It's the warmth that clings to your skin,
Long after the sun sets,
Seeping into your bones,
Making everything feel soft and light,
Like walking barefoot on sun-drenched grass,
Or sipping iced tea while the world hums in the background.

I would tell them love is not just a fleeting moment,
But an endless summer breeze,

A promise that wraps itself around you like the sweetest song,
A melody you hum without even realizing.

It's the feeling of coming home,
A place where you're always welcome,
Where you're seen and heard,
Where every flaw is met with understanding and tenderness.

Love doesn't need to be perfect,
That's what you taught me,
It just needs to be true,
A constant heartbeat in the quiet of the night,
A glow that never fades,
Like fireflies caught in the evening air,
Or the stars that appear after the storm passes.

And I would tell them,
That in you, I've found that love,
A love that feels like the sun,
Always shining, always warm,
Never asking for anything but to be.
But not everyone knows this love right away.
Love doesn't rush,
It waits,
Like the night that appears just before dawn.

For some, it takes time,
It lingers in the quiet spaces between moments,
Waiting for the right moment to bloom,
When it's most needed,
When the soul is open, and the time is right.
Love finds you when you least expect it,

In ways you never imagined,
And it doesn't need to be forced.
It will reach you,
And when it does,
You'll know it was always meant to be.

So, let it come when it's meant to,
And trust that it will,
For love arrives at the perfect time.

And that's what happened when you entered my life.

You were more than a passing storm,
You stayed and made my world light up with color.

My Golden Love

With you, I am weightless.
The world softens, time slows,
and all the noise fades into nothing.
There is no need to be anything but what I am,
because you see me, truly see me,
and still, you stay.

Your name feels like something sacred,
like it was never meant to belong to just this world.
A name that carries stories, that carries fate.
And maybe that's what you are to me,
not just love, but destiny.

Your golden curls catch the light like they were born from it,
spun from the breath of the sun itself,
soft and wild, even untamed,
falling in waves I never want to stop tracing.
There is something about the way they move,
the way they rest against my fingertips,
that makes me believe in beautiful things.

Then there are your eyes,
blue as something endless, something unbound.
They hold the sky, the ocean, the kind of freedom
I have always longed for but never knew how to reach.
And when you look at me, I am not afraid,
not of love, not of falling, not of forever.
Because you are my forever.
You love without hesitation,
without fear, without walls.

Your hands find mine like they belong there,
like they always have.

With you, love is not something fleeting,
not something that comes and goes like the tide.
It is steady, unshaken,
something I can rest in, breathe in,
something I can trust.

I don't need to wonder if this is real.
Because it is real in the way you say my name,
in the way you pull me close without thinking,
in the way your heartbeat quickens when I am near.

You are my golden light,
my deepest ocean,
my safest place.

If this is a story, I pray it never ends.
If this is a dream, I pray I never wake.

Theories Explaining Why People Fall In Love

People fall in love because of chemistry, because of timing, because someone took the wrong turn and ended up in the right place. Because two people reached for the same book, and their hands brushed, and for a second, it felt like fate. Because someone laughed too loudly in a quiet room, and another person found the sound contagious. Because a stranger held the door open a little longer than necessary, and in that small kindness, something unspoken passed between them.

Because some search for the family they never had, while others just want to feel at home in someone else's presence. Because the night feels longer when no one is waiting for you. Because life is unbearably predictable, and sometimes, the only thing that makes it feel spontaneous is an unexpected conversation with the right person at the right time.

Because trembling hands need something steady to hold. Because no one wants to dance alone when their favorite song plays. Because running away gets tiring, and staying still feels easier when someone is standing beside you. Because two people sat next to each other in a classroom years ago, and before they even realized it, their lives had begun to intertwine. Because sometimes, love is just a series of small choices that feel bigger in hindsight.

Because some get lucky. Because others make mistakes that lead them to where they were always meant to be. Because hearts, even when bruised, still beat with hope. Because people need something to believe in, even when they don't believe in themselves. Because someone once wrote a book about a love that survived, and others clung to it, hoping it could be true for them too. Because a song on the radio made someone think of someone else, and suddenly, love felt like something tangible.

Because sometimes, people need someone who sees them for who they could be, not just who they are. Because someone noticed the quiet one who thought they were invisible, and someone else understood the loud one who only spoke that way to hide their fears. Because love doesn't wait for an invitation. Because love doesn't care if someone is ready. Because love isn't always convenient, but it is always transformative.

Because, in the end, people are just stories waiting for the right person to read them.

On Love and Connection

When it comes to love, I have to say: ***do not treat something rare like it is ordinary****. Do not let love become just another thing you pass by. If you find something real, something that sparks light in the dull corners of your heart, do not let it go unrecognized.*

If someone makes you feel something deep, if they inspire you, awaken parts of you that had been dormant, then I hope you have the courage to hold on. Not to grip too tightly, not to possess, but to cherish. Because love, the kind that shifts the ground beneath you, is not something to be overlooked.

We live in a time where love is confused with attention, where fast responses are mistaken for obsession, where people are always looking for something deeper while being too afraid to dive. We've built a culture of detachment, where feelings are hidden beneath sarcasm, where vulnerability is treated as a weakness rather than the foundation of something lasting. We tell ourselves that distance is safer than depth, that caring too much makes us foolish. And in doing so, we rob ourselves of the very thing we claim to be searching for.

But I don't believe in half-hearted love. I don't believe in keeping one foot out the door, in leaving emotions unread, in pretending we don't care when our hearts are screaming otherwise. Love is not meant to be passive.
So, if you find something beautiful in someone, ***tell them****. If someone makes you feel seen in a way the world never has,* ***let them know****.*

Be the person who cares. The one who doesn't play games, who doesn't hide behind indifference, who doesn't withhold love just to appear untouchable. Be the one who risks, who chooses honesty over ease, who sees love not as a transaction but as an offering.

Do not love in halves. Do not give cautiously. Do not let the world convince you that feeling deeply is something to be ashamed of.

Love is not a weakness. Love is not foolish. Love is the bravest thing you will ever do. It is the thing that makes us human, that makes life more than just a series of passing days.

My advice to you is to love fully,
Love wildly,
Love recklessly if you must.
Love like it matters.
Love like you deserve it, because you do.

My dear reader,

Thank you for coming all this way. You have reached the end of our journey and yet love itself has no ending, it only deepens, shifts, and reveals itself in new ways. With my heart in your hands, I thank you for arriving safely, for walking beside me through these pages, for allowing love to be seen through many eyes, many moments, many forms.

From innocent observation to quiet wonder, from shaping an idea to finally understanding its true essence, we have traced love's path together. And now, as you close this book, I hope love continues to find you, in its gentlest embraces and its grandest gestures.

Carry it with you.
Nurture it.
Let it unfold endlessly.
Let love find you.

-`♡´-

About the author

Ariella has always been passionate about creating, whether through painting, drawing, sculpting, or writing. Art is her way of escaping reality and expressing her inner thoughts. A lifelong observer of the world around her, she now shares her perspective and creativity on paper. Outside of her art, Ariella loves animals, enjoys anything sweet to eat, and has a special fondness for both clear weather and the peaceful atmosphere of snowy or rainy seasons. She also loves love and happiness, believing these are things that need to be learned and cherished. Through her work, Ariella wants people to feel these emotions, experiencing the love and joy she seeks to express in every creation.

About the book

There Was Before I Loved You, But Never an After is an observation of love, loss, and human connection. Through poetic storytelling and heartfelt moments, the book takes readers on a journey, capturing the complexities of relationships and the impact they leave behind. With its raw honesty and lyrical beauty, this book speaks to anyone who has ever loved deeply and wrestled with the weight of memories. It is a poignant reflection on how love shapes us: before, during, and long after its presence in our lives.

FSC
www.fsc.org
MIX
Papir fra ansvarlige kilder
Paper from responsible sources
FSC® C105338